Household Food Reminders & Lists

Shopping List

Name:

Name:

Name:

Name:

Pantry Inventory

Item	Quantity	Date

Family Refrigerator Inventory

Item	Quantity	Expiration Date

Family Freezer Inventory List

Item	Quantity	Date

Notes

Shopping List

Name:

Name:

Name:

Name:

Pantry Inventory

Item Quantity	Date

Family Refrigerator Inventory

Item	Quantity	Expiration Date

Family Freezer Inventory List

Item	Quantity	Date

Notes

Shopping List

Name:

Name:

Name:

Name:

Pantry Inventory

Item Quantity	Date

Family Refrigerator Inventory

Item	Quantity	Expiration Date

Family Freezer Inventory List

Item	Quantity	Date

Notes

Shopping List

Name:

Name:

Name:

Name:

Pantry Inventory

Item	Quantity	Date

Family Refrigerator Inventory

Item	Quantity	Expiration Date

Family Freezer Inventory List

Item	Quantity	Date

Notes

Shopping List

Name:

Name:

Name:

Name:

Pantry Inventory

Item	Quantity	Date

Family Refrigerator Inventory

Item	Quantity	Expiration Date

Family Freezer Inventory List

Item	Quantity	Date

Notes

Shopping List

Name:

Name:

Name:

Name:

Pantry Inventory

Item	Quantity	Date

Family Refrigerator Inventory

Item	Quantity	Expiration Date

Family Freezer Inventory List

Item	Quantity	Date

Notes

Shopping List

Name:

Name:

Name:

Name:

Pantry Inventory

Item	Quantity	Date

Family Refrigerator Inventory

Item	Quantity	Expiration Date

Family Freezer Inventory List

Item	Quantity	Date

Notes

Shopping List

Name:

Name:

Name:

Name:

Pantry Inventory

Item	Quantity	Date

Family Refrigerator Inventory

Item	Quantity	Expiration Date

Family Freezer Inventory List

Item	Quantity	Date

Notes

Shopping List

Name:

Name:

Name:

Name:

Pantry Inventory

Item	Quantity	Date

Family Refrigerator Inventory

Item	Quantity	Expiration Date

Family Freezer Inventory List

Item	Quantity	Date

Notes

Shopping List

Name:

Name:

Name:

Name:

Pantry Inventory

Item	Quantity	Date

Family Refrigerator Inventory

Item	Quantity	Expiration Date

Family Freezer Inventory List

Item	Quantity	Date

Notes

Shopping List

Name:

Name:

Name:

Name:

Pantry Inventory

Item	Quantity	Date

Family Refrigerator Inventory

Item	Quantity	Expiration Date

Family Freezer Inventory List

Item	Quantity	Date

Notes

Shopping List

Name:

Name:

Name:

Name:

Pantry Inventory

Item	Quantity	Date

Family Refrigerator Inventory

Item	Quantity	Expiration Date

Family Freezer Inventory List

Item	Quantity	Date

Notes

Shopping List

Name:

Name:

Name:

Name:

Pantry Inventory

Item	Quantity	Date

Family Refrigerator Inventory

Item	Quantity	Expiration Date

Family Freezer Inventory List

Item	Quantity	Date

Notes

Shopping List

Name:

Name:

Name:

Name:

Pantry Inventory

Item	Quantity	Date

Family Refrigerator Inventory

Item	Quantity	Expiration Date

Family Freezer Inventory List

Item	Quantity	Date

Notes

Shopping List

Name:

Name:

Name:

Name:

Pantry Inventory

Item	Quantity	Date

Family Refrigerator Inventory

Item	Quantity	Expiration Date

Family Freezer Inventory List

Item	Quantity	Date

Notes

Shopping List

Name:

Name:

Name:

Name:

Pantry Inventory

Item	Quantity	Date

Family Refrigerator Inventory

Item	Quantity	Expiration Date

Family Freezer Inventory List

Item	Quantity	Date

Notes

Shopping List

Name:

Name:

Name:

Name:

Pantry Inventory

Item	Quantity	Date

Family Refrigerator Inventory

Item	Quantity	Expiration Date

Family Freezer Inventory List

Item	Quantity	Date

Notes

Shopping List

Name:

Name:

Name:

Name:

Pantry Inventory

Item	Quantity	Date

Family Refrigerator Inventory

Item	Quantity	Expiration Date

Family Freezer Inventory List

Item	Quantity	Date

Notes

Shopping List

Name:

Name:

Name:

Name:

Pantry Inventory

Item	Quantity	Date

Family Refrigerator Inventory

Item	Quantity	Expiration Date

Family Freezer Inventory List

Item	Quantity	Date

Notes

Shopping List

Name:

Name:

Name:

Name:

Pantry Inventory

Item	Quantity	Date

Family Refrigerator Inventory

Item	Quantity	Expiration Date

Family Freezer Inventory List

Item	Quantity	Date

Notes

Made in United States
Orlando, FL
22 August 2022

21384248R00057